"Unique and gorgeous in its nakedness. It is a very personal and vulnerable journey through one woman's path from despair to self-knowledge and forgiveness. I can imagine it being a solace to many who wonder how they will get from their pain and double back to a sense of self-love and wonder again. It is the kind of generous book that can accompany you through the worst of times and give you faith that you will find the way...shining through it all is a heart that wants to heal and will help others to do the same. "

- Ann Bradney, Director of Radical Aliveness Institute RAI, Los Angeles, CA

"Coming Up Unstuck is an astoundingly honest story of one woman's transformation—from heart-splitting emotions to joy and integration. Told through prose, poetry, and drawings, Lisa Yvonne cries out in pain, knocks on the door of freedom, and steps over the threshold to become her whole-self."

- Sabra Bowers, Poet/Blogger/Writer, Atlanta, GA

"Using poetry and personal revelation, Lisa Yvonne bravely invites us into her powerful inner journey of self-discovery as she transforms pain into the joy of self-love. Along the way, she beautifully models how relationship often accelerates personal growth."

- Jeff Craft (Kali Das) Founder of Atlanta School of Tantra Yoga and Creator of Ecstatic Relationship®, Atlanta, GA

"Many women find divorce to feel unbearable—worse than death itself—an isolated journey of self-judgment, shame and disempowerment. Lisa does an amazing job of articulating these emotions—in the raw! Lisa Yvonne's vulnerability has become her strength—from which you can draw. Whether contemplating divorce, in the process, or on the other side, allow Lisa to accompany you on the return journey to empowerment, love, and life."

- Lisa Inanna, Holistic Lifestyle Coach, Panama City Beach, FL

"At turns reflective and celebratory, Yvonne's biographical poems and brief personal essays seek to assist the reader in working through universal issues like divorce, grief, and the discovery of a renewed purpose in life. Each emotion is accompanied by elegant black-and-white images by debut illustrator Scott, with additional drawings by the author supplementing her poems. A beautifully illustrated ... collection of poetry and prose."

– Kirkus Reviews

The
Fernhead
Diaries

Coming Up
Unstuck

by Lisa Yvonne

Illustrations by Henry Scott

Publisher's Cataloging-in-Publication Data

Yvonne, Lisa.

Journey through divorce, grieving, and healing. Practice making conscious choices and redefining your relationship agreements. / Lisa Yvonne.

1st edition

p.   cm.

ISBN: 978-0-9982199-0-5

1. Divorce – Grieving – Healing 2. Self-help – Relationship 3. Poetry – Art

306.8 dc23

HQ823

LCCN 2017931461

Fernhead Publishing
P.O. Box 2041
Suwanee, GA 30024

info@fernheadpublishing.com
http://www.fernheadpublishing.com

Printed in the United States of America

Acknowledgments

Many thanks to my former husband, whose journey blended with mine and provided the spring board from which to find myself. Deep appreciation to my children, who continue to teach me to be clear, let go of the voices in my head and be true to myself and authentic in relationship.

Thank you to my siblings and parents, for staying through rocky roads allowing me to emerge, unstuck.

Special thanks to Henry Scott, Deborah Terry, Sabra Bowers, and Linda Wheeler for their many reviews, rereading, and providing critical feedback on structure and support. Thank you to Laurie Davis, for her stalwart faith that everything always works out, and providing clear communication as publicist. Gratefulness to Linda Wheeler beyond measure for her courageous willingness to be there always, and for her patience even when my rebellious child-self takes over. Many thanks to Leslie Rice Parsley for her undaunting stand for my well-being and the plethora of book titles sent to expand my perspective throughout this inquiry, and to Bob Wheeler for continuously pushing me to clear my stories and bring healthiness to all my relationships.

Many thanks to reviewers, enthusiastic supporters and your unwavering belief and love: Jeff Craft, Lee J. and Valorie Howard, Johanna Khati, Rita Lacey, Nina Martin, Kathy Meenach, Regina Merrill, Walter Montero, Sage Morgan, Joye Sewell, and Amy Simms. Abundant gratefulness to Lisa Inanna, my creation partner, helping clear negative spirals and create inner space, clarity and positivity. To all those named and un-named, this book is here because of you.

Healers and Facilitators of Healing: Dr. Bill Bird for his deep support of healthy relationships, Ann Bradney for showing me how to be Radically Alive and opening my heart to love. Gratefulness beyond measure to Susan Austin-Crumpton, Suzy Newman and the Core Star Auric Healing group.

Members of Private Poetry Unveiled and co-authors of *Eggshells of the Soul*: Aarti, Nicole, Phil, Rubina, and Ricardo. PAX volunteers, Rachael and Jan Seigleman, and JaiDei for your tireless efforts on sharing how men and woman can build healthy relationship together. Gratitude for the Hoffman Process and community, and to Landmark Education and community, with their Curriculum for Living, and Team Management and Leadership Programs, providing a foundation for personal growth, responsibility and integrity.

Contents

Foreword

Preface

Introduction

How to Read This Book

Awareness

1. Unconscious Reality
2. Abandonment of Self
3. Reality Defined
4. Internal Expectations
5. Existing Structures
6. Contemplating Divorce
7. Beginning to See
8. Vacillating
9. Stuck in Numbness
10. Grieving
11. Battle-Weary

Consciousness

12. Searching
13. Respite
14. New Road
15. Healing
16. Navigating Rage
17. Being
18. Integrating Forgiveness
19. Gratefulness
20. Choices
21. Releasing
22. Joyfulness

Resources

Foreword

What a journey it has been! Both the actual journey that I was witness to and a supporting player of, which created the poetry and writings of this book, and the unfolding of the creation of this book. What an honor to have been part of both.

Such courage for Lisa to share her journey, exposing vulnerability, which, while scary, is ultimately what leads us all to connection and the knowing we are not alone in this world. Vulnerability, humility, and honesty can be found in these pages. As the book has evolved, the writing has shifted and grown, honoring who Lisa once was and the woman she has become as she has grown into understanding that she has choices and can take ownership and responsibility for her life. As can you.

My hope is that as you read, you are supported and held in your own grief, which is likely what led you to this book. Grief is transient, not permanent, although it can feel as if we will be stuck there forever. Everyone has their own way of grieving, and there is no right or wrong. Give yourself permission to travel your path as only you were meant to, without judgment and without shame. Simply allow.

Safe travels on this journey. Be kind with yourself. Get support. Talk to others. Journal. Cry. Laugh. Allow your life to unfold. In the beginning, it may not look like anything you ever imagined, but that doesn't mean you took a wrong turn. Accept that things happen for a reason and that you may never get an answer to your questions. Grow into the person you were always meant to be. Love who you are.

May you find a kindred soul as you delve into Lisa's poetry and know that you too, will get to the other side of the grief you carry, hopefully to a place of greater intimacy and connection with yourself and others.

—Leslie Rice Parsley, LCSW, RPT-S

HS

Preface

I am writing this book for me. I am writing this book for you.

I am not a therapist. I do not have all the answers. This book is my journey of self-discovery. Your experience is completely your own.

Perhaps, you will find it to be a companion as you awaken to your choices and unique path however your life manifests as you create the environment you desire.

The choices are yours. It is your life to live. You matter.

Wishing you the best on your journey of self-discovery. Thank you for sharing mine.

Introduction

The path

We all have our own journey. Sometimes along the way we discover that our choices no longer serve our vision and that we need to allow the natural cycle of loss and grief to occur so we can clear out the old and invite in joy and new growth.

Phases of awareness

This book has two sections, Awareness and Consciousness.

Awareness is acknowledging where I am in this present moment, regardless of the situation or my judgments, good or bad.

Consciousness is being fully responsible for my choices and owning how my actions affect my world. It is being responsible for what I say and how I participate in life, and then choosing that which serves my highest self.

A small awareness of a behavior or belief can cause a large shift with far-reaching consequences, like a rocket ship flying a single degree off from its course and ending up in a whole new galaxy. In awareness, I make small adjustments and create a world of empowerment and choice rather than reacting and suffering.

Below are some personal examples of my not-so-healthy behaviors and beliefs:

1. Taking care of my partner's needs, but ignoring my own.

2. Speaking my needs, but not holding either one of us in the agreement accountable for the agreements made.

3. Basing my happiness on my partner's happiness.

4. Placing myself second.

5. Blaming others.

6. Being upset with answers and situations that don't meet my expectations.

7. Losing my voice.

The list is endless. These patterns create diminished intimacy and connectedness. Awareness of these patterns is the first step to change.

Seeking

Today I am excited about my journey and the gift of being in this physical body in this time and place. I am no longer waiting in reactivity, but anticipating the next adventure as I flow through this creative process.

Let the journey begin.

I seek to be awake as I walk my path.

BEYOND IDEAS OF

WRONGDOING AND

RIGHT DOING,

THERE IS A FIELD.

I'LL MEET YOU
THERE.

WHEN THE SOUL

LIES DOWN IN THE

GRASS, THE WORLD

IS TOO MUCH TO

TALK ABOUT.

IDEAS, LANGUAGE,

EVEN THE PHRASE

"EACH OTHER",

DOESN'T MAKE

ANY SENSE.

- Rumi

HS

Translation by Coleman Barks

How to Read This Book

Each section starts with a short synopsis, which may include the author's state of being for that particular section and an illustration.

If more background is desired, the second page of each section will include an example or story of explanation for context.

The book is organized in sequential order, so perhaps the first time through, you read in order, to get a sense of the story. But it is not required.

You can pick a section and read only the section that applies to your mood at the time.

You can skip the summary pages and go straight to the poetry, although then you would miss Henry's beautiful illustrations.

You can read only the headlines and then the poetry.

You can look at the illustrations and then the poetry.

You can read the poetry and then go back to the illustrations and summary.

You can skip the poetry and look at the illustrations.

You can skip the context page.

You can read this book in whatever order or however you like.

If you want to immerse yourself in grief immediately, you could start with the section, 'Stuck in Numbness'.

As with your life, it is always your choice.

Note: Primitive drawings are Lisa's art while the beautiful intricate illustrations are created by Henry.

Definition

FERN: a flowerless spore-producing plant; especially: plants possessing roots, stems, and leaf like fronds.

HEAD: the upper or anterior division of the animal body that contains the brain, a: intellect, b: mental qualities, c: mental or emotional control, poise, d: headache. The chief sense organs, including the mouth and ears.

FERNHEAD: Fern + head. Replacing one's head with a fern. Breathing and releasing all thoughts, being still. Allowing grateful joy and listening for what's next from within.

I am not my thoughts. I am my being.

I'm sorry
Forgive me
I love you
Thank you

—Ho 'oh pono pono

HS

Phase 1

Awareness

My eyes are open. I see what is around me. Sometimes I hear my words (either spoken or in my head), and sometimes I do not listen. In safe, far-away places, sometimes I listen to my heart. Sometimes I cannot move.

Contemplating agreements made. Don Miguel Ruiz, author of *The Four Agreements*, writes about how people will take on endless abuse. When either the abuse increases or our understanding of what we will tolerate changes, only then will we allow change in our lives.

Relationships take awareness. I forget to be mindful. Of myself. Of others.

I have the power to leave, so I must also have the power to stay.

I did not know I can be present and have a voice, nor was I aware that we have choices and can always redefine agreements.

1 Unconscious Reality

I grew up believing there was only one model from which to choose.

Sometimes choices are not obvious.

I am learning that I have choices and I am responsible for creating my world.

HS

UNCONSCIOUS REALITY. I decided love hurts. I began building barriers, keeping others at arm's length, and willing myself to be needless. I became a silent chameleon, acquiescing to whatever the situation called for and striving for sainthood.

I stuffed down my emotions and stomped on my individuality as the rage, bitterness, loneliness, regret, and evidence that I didn't matter built up in my body, spirit, and psyche. I created an outer world that reflected my inner state. The reality is, however, that I have needs and desires, even when I choose to be unconscious about them. I am an ordinary human being, not a saint.

The payoff of perceived perfection justified my picking apart my mate and blaming everyone else for the state I was in. Similar to the Pink Floyd song "Don't Leave Me Now," where the singer croons about beating his partner to a pulp on a Saturday night, my patterns of controlling, manipulating, and blaming gave me excuses to build walls of resentment and anger and kept me stuck in a place of miserable survival.

I blamed my choice of a husband on my mother instead of owning that I was attracted to and loved this man and that my higher self put me in this relationship to learn and grow.

The unconscious reality I created by inhaling everyone else's views without discernment gave me no choices, no room to honor myself or anyone else. I was in a stuck place and it was the only thing I knew.

I know now that I was totally responsible for the lack of love and intimacy in my marriage. But at that time it was...

UNCONSCIOUS REALITY.

Whose Dream?

"You should,

it's expected"

"no one else does it that way"

"get married

to a nice boy"

"same backgrounds mix best"

whose dream?

I don't like nice boys.

First Christmas

the stocking is stuffed
  with treats and
    small presents
      packages of joy and hope tied
    symbolically
  recreating the
Christmas that once was

stitches on the reindeer
took three drops of blood
  needle-prick preview
    futile attempts
     foreshadowing
    future

hours of anticipation
sighs of pleasure
waiting...

    this pattern
      starting early
       in the duel
        between us

    flat stocking
    a childhood
    expression
    of wishes
unfulfilled, empty
without thought
  of the other

Time

Time is easing itself
  s l o w l y
   along

seconds

   turning
    to
     minutes

 c r e e p i n g
   c r a w l i n g

toward
eternity.

  abstract
  real
  relative
 perspective

  would not
  exist
  without
 time

Repeating the Cycle

a depressed woman, old
at twenty-five
will be beaten by fifty

and why do we have children
so they can go through the same
misery and confusion?
it doesn't seem right somehow

"Winter" is such reflective music
striking chords
of emotion

harmonic dancing keys
playing a tune on my soul.

what shall I name my baby?

---

[1] "Winter" a song by George Winston

2 Abandonment of Self

Expectations are not a good recipe for trust and intimacy.

Thinking I did not matter offered me no choices.

HS

ABANDONMENT OF SELF. Expectations can kill a joyful situation, especially expectations that are not voiced. My specialty.

My child-self wanted full acceptance and expected my partner to fulfill my dreams, read my mind, and be everything to me. But I did not know that I had to give voice to my wants and needs. I assumed my spouse, my family, and anyone around me would automatically know what I was thinking.

Expectations without voice are not a good recipe for intimacy, trust, and relationship building. Everywhere I turned, I created relationships and evidence which confirmed that I didn't matter.

I went into marriage with the understanding that I would be the sacrificial lamb and would die for the good of the whole. I believed that is what happens in relationship.

On one hand, loving the life I chose, being with my children and participating in community. On the other, suffocating myself by not speaking up and not creating partnership with my husband. I didn't know I could have both, that I could be in a nurturing relationship and maintain my individuality.

Having a mindset that I didn't matter and not understanding that men may want to provide the best for their mate, I took my husband's approach to choosing what he thought was best for me as more evidence of annihilation of myself, not the gift he was trying to offer.

And no matter who I am with, how I interact with others is really up to me. It is my responsibility to honor agreements, recognize my power, and choose how I participate. I don't need to blame everyone else.

ABANDONMENT OF SELF.

First Christmas Coat

desiring
  dignity
    adulthood
      distinguished by
        deep gray
        wool
        coat,
        full
        length

    to show
  the world
    i am grown up,
      a woman now

    instead
    his choice:
    efficient
    all-purpose
    multi-weather
    metallic space jacket
    silver sheen
      without style
        ribbed belt
        wide
        and
        ugly

    like our
    marriage.

Sublet to Myself

my wounds are not so great
if yours are greater

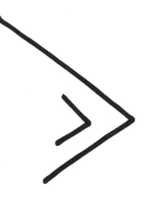

my love is not so necessary
if yours loves better

my thoughts are not so
important
if yours are always
verbalized

the space that requires
me
defining
who you are
is not available

sublet
to myself

Abandonment (of Self)

it starts with
abandonment

it ends
with
divorce

or perhaps…

it starts with
self-discovery

and ends
with

love

I Remember

I remember
drowning
in a sea of oppression

I remember
    hopelessness

I seek to forget
    the way I knew before
    how to survive

abandonment of myself
a disaster for reaching

to excel was to die
    to stand alone was to judge
        all others for their lack of self
        to voice my needs was
            to expose my weakness
            vulnerability
            humanity

to renege on the vow
    would condemn all others

as the paradigm of
    Together
        was their
        only hope of
        salvation

3 Reality Defined

Making myself small did not make me or anyone around me happy.

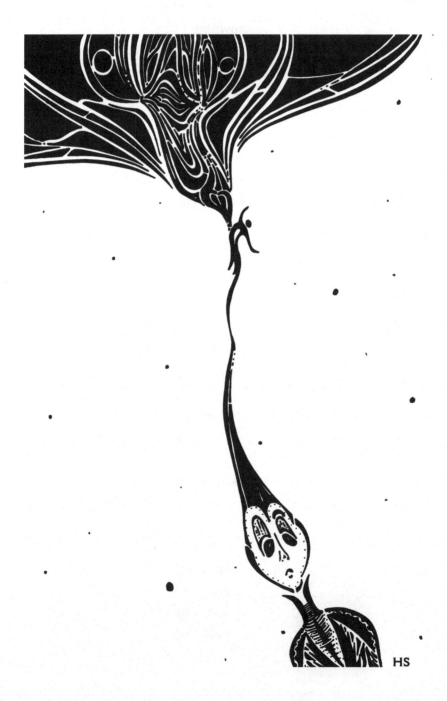

REALITY DEFINED. I gave myself a small space in which to live. I convinced myself that I didn't deserve to take up too much space, use up too much air. It was my destiny to be invisible in the world and insignificant in relationship.

I stood for peace in the house and took full responsibility for everyone else's happiness, but not my own. My complete lack of boundaries enmeshed me in the sorrows of the world. There were no borders between myself and others.

For a long time, I was happy because I loved raising my children and working. Fitting into community, going to church, following the rules, and taking care of everyone else fed me.

As my children became older, I realized I was lonely and depressed, that I had needs and wanted companionship. Changing was difficult because I had no tools, did not know how to receive, and could not see the structure already set up for me to have no needs. Changing was a difficult charter while still holding the belief that I didn't matter and couldn't make a difference.

I shut off parts of myself and did not listen to my internal yearnings. Indeed, I was not even aware of my heart and could not hear it speak. I was unaware that a partnership with my heart was possible. I lived with patterns of denial, running away, and being in pain. Who was I to dare to be happy?

My happiness was dependent on the people around me, not on my own internal compass. At the time I wrote the poems in the Awareness section all I knew was my own living death.

REALITY DEFINED.

Silence

silence like golden
raindrops falling
touching the stillness
gentle like rain
falling softly

yearning
hearts
stilled like trees in the wood
waiting for the logger
to chop them down
still and stoic in their yawning
power of sunlight rings
golden through
the years
as life is cut off suddenly
dancing death shadows
on the wall
there's no one home
to hear my cry
in the
silence
of the morning
in the fall
winter on
the way

how to get
through
another
day
sleeping
awake
and
silent

Wound

A walking open wound

bumping into walls and corners

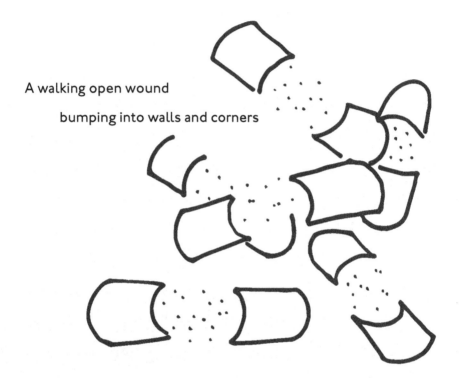

Not a Companion

feeling

  inadequate

    knowing we are all alone

I try to love so much

  but it falls down because

  they're children

    not companions

Spinning in Reality

Spinning, sinking
turning tired
whirling silly
could give a flip
about the math
behind the theory
under the smile
beneath the equation
beside the wall
behind the façade
within the dream
around the bend
and over the hill
regarding one's life
and all the pieces to
be put together
from the puzzle parts

that

fell

on

the

floor

4 Internal Expectations

Suffering inside because I could not live up to a perfect set of expectations.

Who can?

INTERNAL EXPECTATIONS. Continuing to believe I was full only when taking care of others, not realizing I was empty because I didn't value myself. I also rejected my husband in his quest to build a kingdom. My internal agreement of unworthiness, my inability to receive, and perhaps picking a mate with whom I was not able to be vulnerable and cherished, aligned with my belief system that I was nothing.

When I was buying a car, the salesman spoke only to my husband. When neither my husband nor the salesman acknowledged my presence, I shut down instead of speaking up. I didn't know my husband was trying to get the best deal by navigating the world and language of men. His approach validated (again) the vicious cycle of belief in my head that I didn't matter.

Had I been able to articulate this belief at the time, perhaps he would have heard me. My pattern of having no voice was deeply engrained in our dance. In my ignorance of how social structures with men worked, I allowed my marriage and social or business interactions with others to supply more evidence that I didn't matter. I did not know how to connect and create intimacy and partnership.

This next set of poems reflects my emptiness and the expectations that make it seem futile to try to achieve visibility.

INTERNAL EXPECTATIONS.

Hollow Candy

we

are

candies

in a jar

the same

yet variations

abound

empty eyes

happy lips

hollow insides

waiting

searching

following

individual

journeys

and

isolated

in

our

containment

Murky Depths

dreary day
 blankets of soggy
  quilt
   batting
     c o v e r
    the sky

     water cold
      puddle
       yearning
        misty swirling
         macabre dervish
        dance of warm currents
      that
  change the flow
     of the day

       depth
      mirrored by
    shallow
  opaque
   pool

        murky casts of brown
         with oils blues greens
          surreal under the
           surface
            protecting the
             inner
              sanctum
               of the
                soul

Arduous Journey

all grown up
wrinkles on face
hands arms
and lace
so when will I be
who I am?
choices daily to speak
or deny
lessons to learn
music to sing
games to dance

why is it so arduous
this journey we take
will I be alone
does it matter
are the structures real?
for so many they hold
up everything
and people
love
seeing
y
o
u
f
a
l
l

Judas

you didn't follow the rules

you spoke out inappropriately

you're selfish

you're a liar

and a Judas

I could just stay

and keep us

both

miserable

5 Existing Structures

Pretending to fit a model that didn't serve my inner desires.

HS

EXISTING STRUCTURES. Pretending on the outside.

The pull of society is strong. To stand alone is often a fearsome path. I didn't know how to find my way.

I made the decision to leave my husband one Sunday in February. On Monday, my boss announced that the division of the company where I worked was going to be shut down and I needed to start looking for a new job. On Wednesday, I went against a direct request made by my favorite boss who wanted to fire me for insubordination before the lay offs even began.

And I still wanted the divorce. I knew to my core that this was the right decision for me at that time.

I interviewed with the "safe" division of the company and moved to a job with a boss who disempowered anyone who thought differently or was an independent thinker. My outer world now fully reflected my inner state, with my community and safety nets falling apart in every realm. The environments I was in mirrored my belief that I had no value. Again, these things were my own creation.

Every structure I knew and believed was smashed in around me. It was like the movie *Inception*, where the make-believe buildings crash into the sand dunes along the beach.

The external was now reflecting the internal.

EXISTING STRUCTURES.

6:30 A.M.

a thousand steps repetitive
echo in a concrete chamber
chipped burgundy painted stairwell
spilled coffee staining the landing

office door heavy, strain to open
catacomb crypts
dimly shuffling feet move
through dark, hallway of pre-dawn liquid ink
recording no rustlings of living beings
no breathing
no living

row of framed structures without
ceilings or doors, carpeted walls
with openings like gopher holes
padded like an insane asylum
cubbies created
for extraordinary minds
in ordinary constrained
tasks of perpetual perceived
importance (arbitrary)
hungering to
make a difference, yet caught
like a cog without courage
in a cubicle

Puffer Fish

it seems that I
s
p
i
r
a
l
into the mire
while puffer fish
pontificate their importance
and prestige
snuffling, chortling
pompous words
perception of grace profound
wasting my time
as I sit in this line
wanting to break free
from the continuous
barrage
of shit

Weasel's Lair

why do I not care
  that I sit in the weasel's lair
  without enthusiasm
  or fear
      apathetic
        to the
        end
      nor will I bend
    to change the perception
  of my intelligence

      alas, I do not respect
      nor plan to dissect
    the power
    nor will I give it credence
  by acknowledging
this dour
circumstance
of the
boss-employee
  situation

Conference Call Hallway

voices chatter in the pipes
down the hall
speaker phone
squawks loudly as the myriad
egos compete to be heard

justification of existence
abounds in the verbal flowing
of acronyms not knowing
the meaning of why are we here

pretending understanding
creating blockades and withholding
purpose of information I hear
echoes through the wall
black boxes of importance showing
personalities pumped up blowing
fighting stance to always be right

verbal ebb and fall of
unregulated volume
distract the mind
trying to concentrate
feeling within
the game that is played
could stop at any minute

as systems
they shatter.

so does any of it really
matter?

Trap Unsprung

are you threatened?
is your façade so thick
you cannot look within?

are you so miserable that
any difference of opinion
solidifies your core of loathing?

your self worth is
staked on the society
you hate

you set up lies and deceit
to bring others into your
folds of duplicity

wretchedness spreading
according to
your will

And

I am no longer
in your
trap

Bermuda Lawn

large

words

float

around

pompous

important

depicting the
superiority of
colloquialisms
and acronyms

is it useful
or artificial to
keep the masses working
to buy the
American
Dream

and suffocate
in the
Bermuda lawns.

Or is fescue
better?

6 Contemplating Divorce

Perhaps there is a possibility that I can change my agreements.

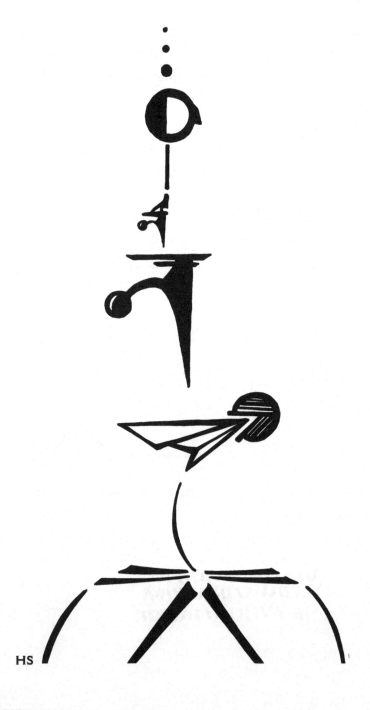

HS

CONTEMPLATING DIVORCE. I took the children to the new mall without showering. I wasn't wearing any makeup or my ring and had not dressed up for outward appearances. As we were standing in line, a man with his two children started talking to me. His kids were encouraging him to give me his phone number. Hmmm, I said to myself. If he found me attractive, then perhaps others might also. Once again, if "they" like me, then there is hope.

I didn't call him, but the microscopic hope that I could have something different fueled my spirit. That single encounter gave me courage to explore my agreements. I was still in my marriage and trying to figure things out. But now I saw the possibility of choice. This was also the day that I bought *The Four Agreements* by Don Miguel Ruiz.

In the meantime, I continued to live within the belief system where it felt normal and appropriate for me to not have any value or worthiness. I had no tools to help me take ownership of my own space, breath, or body.

At that time, I was still blaming my father for leaving when I was a teenager (sorry, Dad) and still choosing to be the door mat instead of the aggressor or to have feelings (sorry, Mom). Surely it must be healthier, I thought, to stifle emotions. This was a conscious unconscious decision. I knew of no other model and did not know I could create my own way and have a say in how my life goes.

I started thinking about divorce. In my mind, it was the only option. Since I blamed everyone else for my unhappiness, then it must be my husband who was the cause of my unrest. Perhaps, I thought, I must leave.

CONTEMPLATING DIVORCE.

Commitment and Loyalty

spiraling into the abyss
of unconsciousness
blackness of
consequences
yet to be rendered

how to break this cycle
without breaking my world
and the structure upon
which my children
my husband
and I rely

commitment and loyalty
two attributes
cherished
risking
hypocrisy
by breaking a
promise

live or die
my torture or my death

how will I know the way?

Acting

I know the choices in my head

the hard part is

acting

Converge

how to reconcile the

choices of my current state

with what I think I want

create a new

environment

converging

with

agreements

broken

affecting

others

can I just wake

up tomorrow and

be done?

Choices

why didn't you tell me

there were choices?

7 Beginning to See

I am learning that my baggage of no self-worth colors my world.
Teaching others to not care for me creates a forlorn and lonely place.
I need to be fed.

BEGINNING TO SEE. I brought baggage and unconscious patterns into my marriage. Setting up expectations and never giving myself a choice or a voice, I became lost in my head. I couldn't even hear my husband over the noise of my own stuff.

Long after the divorce, I discovered the many ways in which I had trained my husband to not care for me. When we were first together, I was running in the neighborhood and was out longer than expected one night. He got in his truck and drove around looking for me because he was worried.

What did I do? Did I thank him for caring? For looking for me? No. I yelled at him that I could take care of myself and said, "Don't ever do that again!"

Well, he didn't. He didn't ever look for me again. Ever.

The man I was married to never knew what hit him when I finally decided that I mattered. He loved me. And I didn't remember this for a long time, but I loved him, too. I was so wounded, stuck, and unable to receive that I never let him in, nor did I ever share myself fully. Or perhaps I didn't pick a man who could honor me for who I am. Instead, I felt I had to change to accommodate him to maintain peace in the house. I had to use my internal defense mechanisms of distance to prove that I could be independent from his strong personality.

I was learning to be aware of who I was at the time. Aware of my feelings. Aware of myself. Aware now of the impact of my changes and choices on everyone in my world. My husband. My children. Myself. The cost of not valuing myself.

BEGINNING TO SEE.

He Said, She Said

"What do you want?"
   "I want a treadmill."
      and a stair-stepper
         climbed into the room.

"What do you want?"
   "I want a treadmill."
       a rowing machine floated in.

"What do you want?"
   "I want a treadmill."
      a mass of springs and pulleys
        weight compelled
        hard seat lacking
          comfort
            manual
          training
        system
      stalked into the room,
    taking root.

"What do you want?"
   "a treadmill."

"A tread mill?"
　　"a treadmill."

　　　　"for my
　　　walk of life
　　　journey
　　　sharing
　　　parallel paths
　　sheltered from
　　the elements
　　band of black
　　　moving to my step
　　　cushioned
　　　arms round
　　　　for protection
　　　balance
　　　holding"

"When will you run?"
　　"When you're not."

"What do you want?"
　　"To be far, far away from you
　　forever.

Uncertainty

attempting to figure out
math and logistics
reconnaissance
mapping for
control

nothing fits

I am terrified of the uncertainty

I don't want to hurt my
children
myself or
him
but I cannot continue to
live with the events of
the day

I want to be aware
in my attraction
I wasn't conscious before
I want it to be summer
after the war.

8 Vacillating

My pendulum swings between status quo and changing my agreements.

HS

VACILLATING. Teetering between being fine with the status quo and glad to have my family, house, job, and all the accoutrements of a successful life, or giving up on myself, blaming, and remaining unhappy, angry and suffering. I was not in a place where I realized that I could actually have a voice and stay in relationship.

Knowing now, responsibility is all mine, I create my environment.

Now embracing the belief that I re-created childhood drama in relationship, I am finding healing as an adult. According to *Getting the Love You Want: A Guide for Couples* by Harville Hendrix, it doesn't matter how loving your parents are. No one person can ever fulfill all the needs and expectations of another human being. Each individual, regardless of their background, may struggle with the universal issue of (un)worthiness, a sense of shame, or of not being enough; for others, this concept is not even in their realm of consciousness.

My pendulum continues to swing between status quo and changing. i.e., for me, this meant getting a divorce. Not realizing the choice to have a voice was mine all along, and realizing later that if I had the option to leave, I also had the choice to stay, I didn't give myself permission to own my power. It was easier to condemn myself to a world of no acknowledgement. That was my punishment for living.

I read the book *Too Good to Leave, Too Bad to Stay* by Mira Kirshenbaum multiple times. I made spreadsheets and checklists and double and triple checked. Answering yes to ninety percent of the questions that said to go, I had to read the book again and again, just to make sure, before I broke my world and the world of my children and husband apart.

VACILLATING.

Leaky Wife

leaky pen
 leaky life
  leaky wife
   leaky strife
   blots on the page
   turn into matter and
   nothing is turned
   into something symbolic
  but I know not what I write
  only that language and
  predefined shoulds
   stand in the way
    of feelings that
    pervade and abound
   in my
  heart, chest, soul
  and mind.

Father-Daughter

could it be

the lack of

father-daughter

relationship

that causes the

consternation?

the loss

the void

maybe it's not

husband-wife

that is the culprit

Suffocating

is it true
that life begins at thirty?
defining searching
conforming to society's mold
tried and true
didn't work for me
screaming for release
to get out of this hold
suffocating, pressure
on my lungs
collapsing
get me out of this box
before it goes into the
ground forever
with worms rotting
fungus growing
mold gathering
immobilized by fear
and expectations
that will be torn
from all that seems
is not real
only my pending death will
motivate me away
from the constrictive
boards pressing against
my face

get out! run away!

Balloon Dancing

balloon dancing
  my son jumping joyfully
  from couch to chair
a knight avoiding the alligators
  on the floor
  my daughter giggling
  a princess
    sliding to the next
      precariously tipping pillow
  exuberant laughter bubbles
  in the living room
  Indigo girls playing "Closer to fine"

    being present
    is a
  wonderful
  gift

    thankful for
      their vessels that
        fill me up and make
          me feel trite at the
            nonsense going through
            my head

  I turn thirty-seven today.

Rinse, Repeat

rhythmic
   cycles
      stand
         breathe
         work
       sleep
      walk
     wonder
   rinse
repeat

  evolving awareness
  focus shifting

    despair over parental issues
      compete and conquer the challenges
       of marital issues

  acquiescing to the benefits of being married

  changing

  at a moment's notice

  rinse
  repeat

Speak Up

deceptions so subtle
    just a little lie
        here and there

    don't use me as your excuse
    when you don't want to go
    have clarity
    stand up

    although
  easy
to say

as
my
myriad
excuses
spill
into
the void

blah
blah
blah

blaming you
I can't seem
to stand up
for
myself

Cadence

crinkly velvet chaise rests beneath
my thighs and back as thoughts trail
lazily around the
labyrinth of my mind
experiencing
sadness and joy
exquisite
simultaneously

how precious life is
how soon our bodies age
and I've no one to share
these patterns of growth

these moments of lucidity
with
anyone other
than my children
my brother
my sisters
my mother
my father

how long can they continue
to hear the same thing
adjusting to
my cadence
of repetition
before they, too,
say enough of your
silliness!

be gone!

9 Stuck in Numbness

I am lost forever. No one knows how to get me out.

I am stuck in loss of love, life, and happiness.

My grief crashes into my body
and permeates my soul.

HS

STUCK IN NUMBNESS.   I saw myself as lost forever, no one knowing how to get me out, and me not being aware even if they tried.

I learned later that I am the only one who can get me out. I am the only one who can make choices for me.

It took several years to allow the grief of the years to come crashing in and around me. It took several more years to wallow in it and actually let myself feel it.

I went to Los Angeles the week before the September 11, 2001, Twin Towers attacks in New York, so I could get counseling from my brother on what to do and how to say my piece. We had made a pact at age ten that we would break the pattern of divorce in our family. We would do it differently. I requested permission from my brother to renege on our agreement.

On my return, dealing with the grief of the world after the bombings of the World Trade Center, and the subsequent death of the teenage son of my dear friend, led to my decision that I could no longer contribute to the suffering of the world, by staying in this place of sorrow.

I finally allowed the physical world to ground me in grief rather than exiting my body and escaping into my mind and flying far beyond the present. I finally acknowledged my destitution as my own and not a projection of someone else's pain.

The grieving begins. I am lost in the contemplation of grief. I am still not able to fully own it or live it emotionally, but in my mind I am getting ready to go into the tunnel of death, not knowing if I will return.

STUCK IN NUMBNESS.

Doll in the Attic

the doll
  disappeared for forty years
    she couldn't move
      she was frozen in time
        while her family
          petrified
        by sorrow and the terror of losing
      themselves
        chose to
          abandon her in the
            attic where no others
              had gone
          for forty years
      afraid of what they might find
      in themselves
        dolls we are
          we didn't know we could
            laugh
                or cry
                  or live
                    or die

to be shaped by fear
  impending doom
    abandonment of self
    love of life
      squeezed out drop by bloody drop
  lifeless in the carpet reddish
  brown and rusty
    with the sound of the
      bird singing outside
        and the tea set broken
        in the garden
          lost

Taffy

how come
action
is so
difficult?

moving
like
taffy

when the choices seem obvious

fear or
limbo

waiting or
stagnating

timing? or
just plain
scared

who knows

the futility
of
it
all

In-Flight

I wish I had a notebook
to write down all my thoughts
instead of an airplane napkin
with peanut salt on it
dusty

reflections in the glass
through the sunset
with the plane flying
into blue air space
or clouds

lives en route
on hold
in between
encapsulated in this compartment
thinking about nothing
while the world races beyond
to oblivion
chattering television
mindless safety precautions

put your air mask to your face first
before helping others

welcome aboard, ma'am
how is your day?

my what?

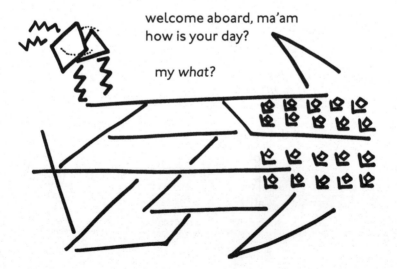

Weary World

arbitrary situations
lacking definition

circles of uninterrupted
work

faces of unemployed,
working or sleeping are all
the same
without rest from the
weary world
of pretend

glowing embers
of competence sputter
out quietly one by one
as midnight blackness
overtakes them

One Tunnel

my heavy heart lightens
grief is lifted for
a moment

maybe for a day

or several

too much to ask,
  for a week?

consequences of my choices
will strike again

        why didn't the
        instruction book work?

        how to make choices when
        there is only

        one

10 Grieving

Life, death, life cycle.

I allow the grieving to begin. The floodgates pour open, beginning the cleansing of my soul.

GRIEVING. Life, death, life cycle. Our society prefers quick fixes. We don't allow time for grieving, which is a vital step toward healing, growing, and creating. Nature destroys and the earth lies fallow before life begins growing again. Why don't we follow these cycles, too?

Falling into the knowing of my choices. Speaking and causing of my own voice to emerge.

This stage of grieving is crucial to healing. Whether I choose to stay in my relationship, lose the relationship, or make any kind of change, I need to grieve for the loss of what was, either real or perceived.

Grieving cleanses. Wipe clear the slate. And from nothing, I can create anything.

During my grieving cycle, I asked permission from those I loved and respected if it would be okay for me to change things. I asked my pastor at the time. May I get divorced? It went against my deeply engrained inherent loyalty and commitment to promises made.

My soul's heaviness permeated my every experience. My friend Kathy gave me a book called *How to Survive the Loss of a Love*, by Harold H. Bloomfield, Melba Colgrove, and Peter McWilliams, which focuses on loss caused by death, divorce, or breaking up. Her gift helped me know it was okay for me to be stricken by grief and that one day I would move beyond it.

GRIEVING.

Killing Field

sadness expands in my psyche
my physical being
saturated with loss
swollen with regret
and weeping

I did not know
how to fit into
this fold

why was it kept silent
this blind following
into the killing field
the shearing of
individuality
for the
sake
of a
vow

how many of us
facing tombs
see hope in
graveyards
of the past
with eyes alive
and lives full
of emptiness
hollow
ready to
be shorn
without realizing
that life is short
and then you die

Cored

I want to be healthy

how do I continue
the search
when all around me is
death and destruction

the hollowness
cores me like an apple
cut through the middle

oops - you're dead

Bruises of the Soul

black

  violet

    purple

      blue

despair

  seeps

    into my soul

      as the realization

        that the

          tomb

            I have created

          has

    c   r   a   c   k   e   d

      who I am

  my eyes fill

  with the ache

  of longing

    knowing the

    immersion of

  sorrow

is inevitable

Resounding Thunder

learning I really do care for him
   but it is too late as I continue my path of
D E S T R U C T I O N

physical manifestations
chest stomach body back
expanding exploding continuous
heartbeat tormenting constant
   aching to the marrow
   of my bones

the depth of
devastation
startles me

as exponential
growth of
agony and
creating
hurt in others
is endless

the reality of making
the right choice for me deafens
my ears and heart with resounding
thunder, I cannot think washing
through the rumbling boom
and torrential tide
of feelings

Terror of Indifference

each breath inhaling
embers
dust
murky air
particles
burn the lungs

choking
on the inhalations
of
living

fingers creeping
tight over
throats
terror of indifference
stains the ground
with the brown
curdled
scream of
nothingness

11 Battle-weary

I am tired.

My grieving continues beyond my wildest imagination.

Ideals shattered, my family is in the path of destruction.

HS

BATTLE-WEARY. The grieving continues beyond my wildest imaginings. The depth of emotion seems endless. I am grieving the abandonment of self, the loss of ideals, the shattering of my family. The structure within society, the family built with my consent, my creation and my blessing is now being destroyed.

The world continues to revolve and function around me, and inside I am screaming as I am heavy with responsibility and future choices.

Barely able to function at work, I rely on my reputation for excellence to carry me through this time of total annihilation of everything I know and love.

Loss of love, loss of family, loss of job.

I know in my heart of hearts that the decision is already made. I have permission from my brother, from my pastor, from my friends. I never before realized that I also needed to receive permission from myself. Now I am acknowledging the change of inevitability and understanding that I never allowed myself to be fed physically, emotionally, intellectually, and spiritually. I am accepting I was not willing to do the work to keep this marriage alive. And that I am responsible for this madness.

My teacher, Susan Austin-Crumpton, says suffering is the survivor self's defense mechanism to stay stuck in known or familiar pain, while grieving or feeling pain from an event or situation is part of the human condition. It is the suffering that we create in our heads from expectations not being met that causes us the most pain. And it is self-inflicted.

We can either allow the pain of not getting what we want or we can suffer when the answer is not what we want. Two very different perspectives.

BATTLE-WEARY.

Growing Grief

lying prostrate
naked

pushing the day
away
  I want to hide
    and sleep
   or fly
  to
fantasyland

    yet obligations
   responsibilities
  kick within
and force
    me to move
     into
   the world
paste a smile
   and chat
    at coffee

as stomach acids churn

boiling, rolling nausea,
fear, uncertainty, and grief

grow
deep
within

Silent Screaming

sea of faces
situations
disconnected
a report
flash of
recognition
in eyes
not dead

surge of light
colors
unrecognizable
sinking slowly
murky
soiled
tar pit swamp
submersing me
struggling
to suck in air
screaming silently
anguished moans
broken only by

"Good morning,
how are you?"

"Fine, thanks."

as the beat of
shattered
expectations
pounds my chest
surreal sorrow
taking over

Alchemy

choking
dust dulls
the senses
impervious to
the need for
clean air
I am weary

lifting my fork
body weight leaden
did alchemy metamorphose
stainless steel tongs
to iron?

"Hello", a burden,
"how is your morning?"
a journey
not to be
traveled

irregular meetings
to discuss more meetings
while I lie dying
in my soul

wrenching muscles
pumping mildly
futilely
dying

Heavy Heart

to get up
  is monumental
    to speak
        requires the effort
            of giants

    let me languish in solitude
    disappear from the world

    my heart hangs heavy
        with the pressure
            of the pending decision
            mourning for family
                ideals
                myself

    walking exhausts
        my limbs
          misery
            overflows
              as my
              eyes
            shed tears
          unmercifully in
    God's house

      carrying
        suffering
          years
          bearing
        down
      on
    my
being

Patterned Abuse

majestic words
   such rationalism
      the prerequisite
         to earthquakes
            opening chasms
            consuming
               destroying

how we can talk
about houses and furniture
time with children

s   p l   i   t   t   I   n   g

my world is
torn apart

I trust seams will be resewn
let God thread the needle

relinquish
   allow all
      emotions
         trust in
            beginnings
            endings

although my view is cloudy
the journey progresses
marked
by God's arms
and the years of
patterned abuse

Eggshells of My Soul

the eggshells of my soul
crinkle at your fury
sounds of anguish
palpable rage
expelling endless
exposure
escaping
from your lips
Whoosh
like a bird
features back
wings drawn in
as I

take on all your sorrow

little did I know
it was you
speaking for my pain

blind
I could not feel
the me

cowardly in a corner
shaking
wanting to leave
this behind

but it is with
me
Still

HS

Phase 2

Consciousness

Contemplating agreements made. Making choices. It doesn't mean I will never again be reactive. I am triggered in a second. The difference is how I choose to handle situations.

Being conscious also does not mean being perfect, and who defines perfect, anyhow? Perhaps perfection is allowing the full human experience including all emotions, instead of shutting down or denying parts of myself to please other people.

I belong in my own skin because I am here, not because I have to do something to be valued. My ears are open. I practice hearing my own voice. I am learning I am safe and can open my heart.

I "re-member" who I am and honor my divinity, your divinity. Our paths together.

12 Searching

Asking myself, what is my passion? What do I want in life? Why am I here?

Hope and seeking are dancing back into my vocabulary.

I breathe, think, and live again.

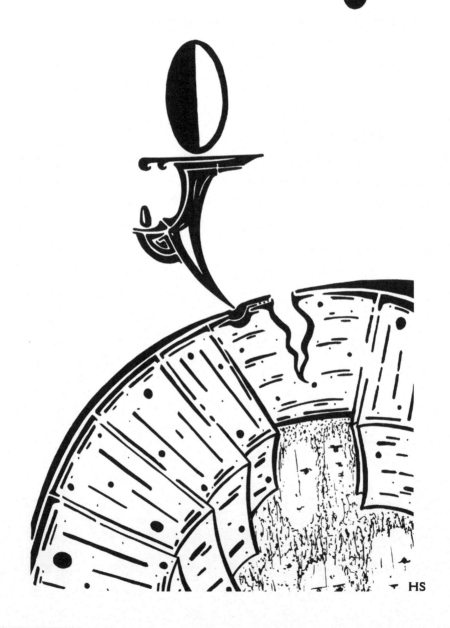

HS

SEARCHING. The eternal hope lives within us as human beings. Wanting to acquire tools to manifest the world I want. Wanting to believe in something larger than myself. Wanting to have purpose in the world and believe there is a reason for existence.

Even as I am stuck in my paradigm of society's expectations, my own self perceptions, the anticipations of the world, my church, my family, and myself, I considered myself a seeker. Yet without sharing this with others, the only person who knew I was seeking was myself. To all outward appearances, I was a mute, docile citizen, behaving as I thought I should.

I recently heard the saying, "Don't should on yourself."

I look back and see that I was a prisoner in a cage of my own creation who saw a pie slice of daylight sky. I didn't know the door was unlocked and I only had to step out, just like Evey in the movie *V for Vendetta*. She accepted her situation so wholly, she didn't even try to escape, and her jail was truly her façade. We trap ourselves, and we can release ourselves as well.

Uncertain of the future, I am capable and willing to move forward in my path. Hoping and seeking are once more dancing into my vocabulary.

Able to breathe, think, and live again, I am on the road to mending, defining, seeking and finding.

SEARCHING.

Escaping Mediocrity

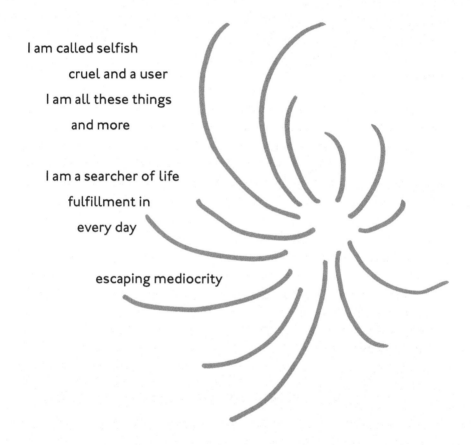

I am called selfish
cruel and a user
I am all these things
and more

I am a searcher of life
fulfillment in
every day

escaping mediocrity

Consequences

doubt creeps in
    fear pervades my
      being
      tenuous
    pondering the
unpredictable

future

  changes made
on a daily basis
  lead to big

CONSEQUENCES

I shall
continue
making choices

Searching

wind caressing me lovingly
     earth solid under my feet

body taking every pleasure
     given in this life
     engaging fully

without reserve
as
life blood courses through my veins

days go by
     physicality and my environment
a constant reminder of this body I am in

essence contained in this form unique
searching

Passion

my spirit
   is
      soaring
         over oceans emerald

as I gaze out from the window seat high in the sky
I see dots of thriving mammals
grazing below

plots of squares
circles of irrigation
feeding the
earth
my body
my spirit

plane landing
me landing
grounding
touching
lives
yearning
crying
laughing
speaking
silence
loving
acceptance

Explore

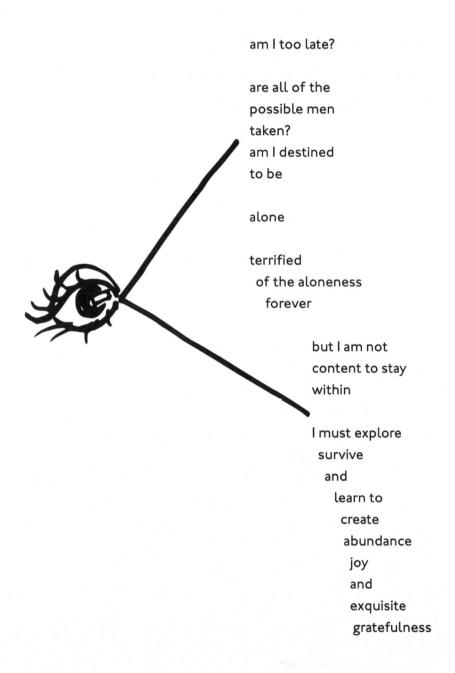

am I too late?

are all of the
possible men
taken?
am I destined
to be

alone

terrified
 of the aloneness
   forever

but I am not
content to stay
within

I must explore
 survive
  and
   learn to
    create
     abundance
     joy
     and
     exquisite
     gratefulness

Good in Growth

I know there
is good in
growth but
at what point
do I stop?

when is enough?
what is happiness?
Is it futile?
will it be all
for
naught?

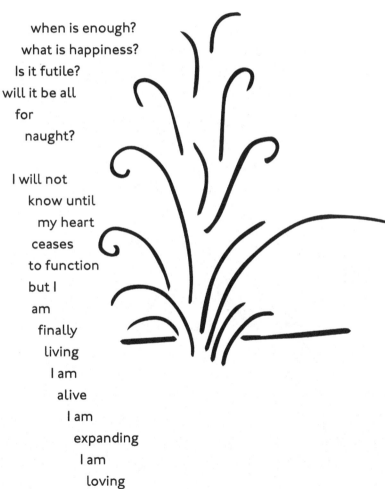

I will not
know until
my heart
ceases
to function
but I
am
finally
living
I am
alive
I am
expanding
I am
loving

13 Respite

I rest and allow time to be.

I am still, sitting peacefully.

It is lovely being alive and nurturing my spirit.

RESPITE. Taking baby steps. Learning I am alive. I breathe and cry. Learning that making the choice to have a voice has not killed me. I am still functioning.

Allowing time for quiet space, being still, sitting peacefully. Sitting with my cat, nurturing my plants, watching fish swimming in their aquarium.

I give myself permission to take a break from the world and my thoughts. I walk and breathe in fully. Fresh air fills my being. Attempting to learn gardening, getting on my bicycle, feeling the exhilaration of the wind cleansing my mind, body, and spirit in joyous aliveness.

Nurture and rest

Laugh and be grateful

Set boundaries

Now with my children grown, sometimes I get into busy mode and fill up every minute of every day, spending evenings out meeting new people, taking classes, and traveling over the weekend. Even if I am doing things I love, it is also important to say no. I need to stay at home and rest. Or read a book. Or nap.

Learning that if my energy level and emotional state are spiraling downward, I need to do something I love or rest. Listen to my favorite music, eat an ice cream cone, be still so I can relax and revive. Spend time with family and friends. I get so used to *doing* that I forget to just be.

Barry Stevens says in *Don't Push the River, It Flows by Itself* that as soon as she starts explaining, she is no longer present. So I take a respite from myself and my thoughts and become present.

RESPITE.

Doing Nothing

salt
water
a teardrop
full and thick
trailing the narrow slope
of the bridge
between my nose and cheeks

rolling
   losing mass as
      it hangs
         gripping the edge
           of my chin

spattering into
a thousand particles
soundless

a pleasant interruption from the day
hearing myself think and talk
without a response

alone

enjoying the comfort of myself
my children
my home
my choices

glad for the time to do nothing

Cacophony

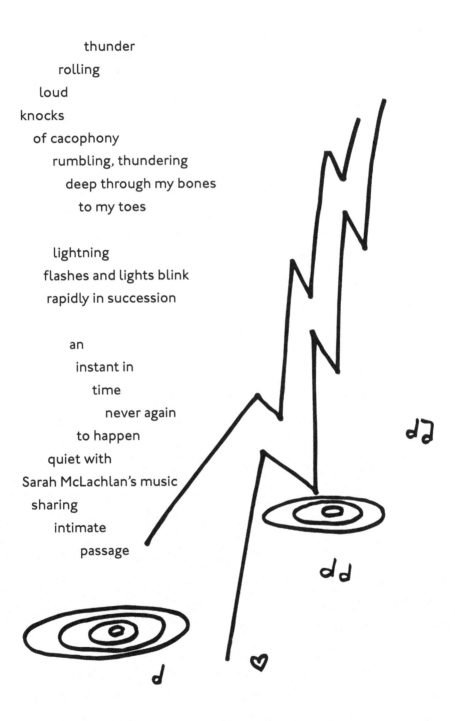

thunder
rolling
loud
knocks
of cacophony
rumbling, thundering
deep through my bones
to my toes

lightning
flashes and lights blink
rapidly in succession

an
instant in
time
never again
to happen
quiet with
Sarah McLachlan's music
sharing
intimate
passage

Golden Bird

desires
  beyond
    square angles
      surrounding
        the world maze

forgetting the old way
  path finding
    looking for a new door
      like a new-born sky
        opening to reveal
          a winding trail

intuiting the
    pre-existence of the
        golden bird flying in the sun
            wing span glorious
                catching the breeze

coming to understand why "should" is a
word best banned from the dictionary

    gaining
      freedom
        consciousness
          self

Respite

my children, my loves
   their smiles precious
      temporary gifts that allowed me to delay
   looking at myself
  and the uncertainty of
not knowing

        do we ever know?
       façade of control lost

facing the endless
   stream of emotions and chatter
     that won't go away

  I wait
   in stillness
   and pray

    for the
      next opportunity

  and learn
   how to become
  a respite from myself

Remembering

Lungs full, body sensations a luxury to feel
with the ground beneath our feet dry
and buildings stable, trees rooted in place
no earth tremors shaking our world
sameness of days a monotony of life, not respected or precious
held dear

forgetting
families a phone call away
or in the next room or on the couch beside me
instant message, a text, a smile
touches the heart of our lives

forgetting
fragile fragments lost in future ponderings
creating meaning
repetitive ritual

long journey, endless night, no reprieve
how to be today?
to spend the hours
that are stretched into forever
and shorter than a whisper
gone with a dandelion puff
forgetting breath of body
re-membering
  gratefulness of experience
    compassion for others
      living this grace gift within

14 New Road

I listen to myself and value my relationship with me.

Perhaps I can entertain sharing with another?

HS

NEW ROAD. I can be in healthy relationships with others when I am in a healthy relationship with myself. A quote from one of my daughter's favorite novels, *The Perks of Being a Wallflower* (1999) by Stephen Chbosky says, "We accept the love we think we deserve."

It sounds so simple, and changing the belief of not deserving to deserving is all it takes. To value myself wherever I am without judgment is difficult. Until I decide to *just do it.*

Sometimes when I am fitting into what I think is successful and I match my surroundings, then it is easy to believe I have value. It is more difficult to maintain my value, my enoughness when I am making mistakes, am shamed or perhaps have a different opinion than others. To stand alone and have value regardless of others' or my own opinions.

It is a conundrum. So if I have judgments and believe only parts of me are "good" and therefore valuable, then I am constantly attempting to find balance between what is good and what is bad. If I am good in my own head and that definition contrasts with someone else's view of value, then my good is now bad, and I am "bad" in the vicious cycle of value. The key is to integrate and embrace all of me. My good and my bad, and to stand in my wholeness.

I am here for a reason. It is okay to take up space. I do not have to *do* anything to earn the right to live. I can just *be.*

I am learning to allow my passions and hopes to surface. And I am giving myself permission to live.

NEW ROAD.

Value

at what point
    did it become clear
      that I had value?

        universal purpose
      spreads before me
     like a painting splashed with color
  a sunrise-pink mango delicious cherry-red juicy

 vivid warmth
   patterns striking and clear
   simple objects shine with clarity

air permeates my existence, expanding permission to live

   trust
    it says quietly

    fifteen minutes at a time are
    all that are required

    rest
     in gratitude

New Road

time
　　travels
　　　slowly
　　　　around
　　　the
block

I wake up ten years later
　　hair gray
　　aching back stiff
　　wondering
　　what happened?
　　how did I arrive at this place?

　　promises shattered
　　as I emerge from the
　　　　nightmare of destruction:
　　　my life
　　　of no voice
　　　no needs
　　　no choice

book unravels
　　ragged seam
　　　　pages torn
　　　　　fluttering
　　　　　gracefully

this story done
　　gathering strength
　　　for the new road

Fresh

learning about my voice
 I dared not
  write in my book
   of dreams as
  I was
 in the process of
              tearing
          down
           structures
         built
        with
       my
      consent

          faithfully following old patterns
        was not be a good start
     for dreams

now
  releasing
    burning rubbish
      clearing space

        placing
      a solid
     groundwork
    for setting boundaries
   forging a bedrock
    a cornerstone
   moving
      f o r w a r d
      fresh

Uncluttered

shredding papers

sorting stacks sales receipts data notes bills and such

swipe off clutter and

wipe clear the surfaces

the daily

memories

the stuff

as I clean out my office

clear the surfaces

open my mind

to new

experiences

uncluttered

My Path

thirty years, more
or less,
hungering
to beat the
lines on
my hands
struggling
they are
life-line short
and split
romance deep
yearning
fulfilling my
deepest desires

figuring out
understanding
dawns
room washed in
crystal shimmering
Light
fear receding
clarity
sinks in
seconds
run trembling
through my fingers
planet spinning
awareness
of
my
path
to
joy

15 Healing

I am healing and my emotions flow through me.

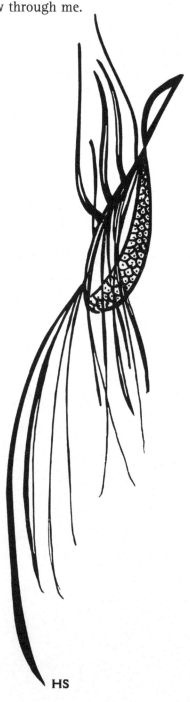

HS

HEALING. The more I heal, the more I know there is more that needs to heal. I peel the onion of my life and discover that the more responsible I am for embracing all my emotions and allowing the ebb and flow of together and separate, the more I heal and the more my emotions reveal.

I recently completed the "Auric Energy" class at The Estuary in Nashville, Tennessee. The first year, we shared our stories and went deeply into trusting the group and learning about ourselves. The second year, we learned about our shadow selves, owning and integrating the darkest pieces within instead of trying to stuff them down. The third year, we learned to hold our integrated selves straight and full and to allow love to come into our selves and know that we are enough.

I embrace all aspects of me, dark and light. And when all of me is honored, I am whole and complete, both unconsciously and consciously. I am aware, one with myself.

I am learning that even when I am vulnerable and needy, even when I overeat or become too busy, that I am perfect, whole, and complete and I am okay. Alanis Morissette's song "I Will Be Good" validates my feeling that no matter what, I will be good.

Embracing my enoughness and humanity, I accept and embrace yours.

HEALING.

Worthiness

erasing society's
expectation of who to be
and masking the fraudulent view
of inadequacy

is an enduring chore
that I intend to be rid of

creating instead
worthiness
wholeness
allowing all
emotions
kindness
to me
and
you

Crashing

crashing through the branches in my mind
storms beat my head against the rock
solid unyielding unforgiving
massive in its solidity

creating new patterns of conscious choice
I plant my feet like tree trunks in the sand
deep into the soil my legs grow
grounding me deep in the mother
as I connect to my yearnings
again

stumbling no more
meandering complete
solitude of gratitude
realizing the sweetness of being
alone with my salvation
bending and swirling
with organic
changes
of the
tide

Never Done

thermometer

```
  \ | /
- pops -
  / | \
```

with food still raw

Is it done yet?

work, still...
patterns and reactivity
abound
           Is it done yet?

growth... again

continuous resolution of Self

am I done yet?

creating drama
       "I've been here before."

               voracious
       cycle   of
       internal   lies
       chatter   this
         act   of
       pretension   temporarily
        putting   myself
           out of   the circle

I stop now
     this mode
          of operandi
     perceiving
          as this pattern completes
responsibility fully mine

     enlightened with
          understanding
               creating forgiveness
               choosing self love
               as I
          give it up
          again

     heart beating
I continue to
     evolve

Reborn

rejuvenation as
my flippers take
me far into the
ocean of forgiveness
free and clear of
clingy tenacious

tendrils
escaping
releasing
as I float into the depths
of the unconscious
light streaming through
green air bubbles
rising to the surface
school of triangle fish dart
in the shadows
cast by cloud ripples
and swoop
gone again
in an
instant
alone
but are we?

cherishing this breath
this growth
this stretching
this connecting

what am I supposed to learn today?
how do I stay with myself?
learn to be with others?

Needs

what do I need?

compassion
   sans judgment
   of self
   or others

strength
intelligence
vulnerability
allowing
accepting

sharing space
companionship
love
nurturing
expansion
joy
laughter
integrating

I need to be able to speak my vulnerabilities
without shame and without feeling like I am
inadequate

Communication

the more I learn

about communication

the more I learn

I need to

be quiet and listen..

to be still.

to listen...

and

hear

my

son

daughter

self

partner

brother

sister

mother

father

colleague

others

16 Navigating Rage

Learning rage cleanses.

I remove judgments of strong emotions and find my fury.

The boiling froth turns into a whisper and is a reminder for me to keep my voice.

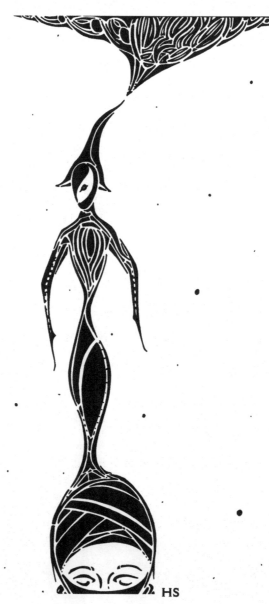

RAGE. I didn't know I had rage. I knew I was angry, but rage? Even though I made my choices and created the life I wanted, I still had emotions bubbling deep inside me that I did not understand. I discovered it when I quit blaming the man I married, and everyone else around me. My rage was my own and directed at me as well as at everyone else in the world.

My view of his fatherhood became more generous after I left him. All I could see through my tunnel vision while in the marriage was an ogre that covered up the divine within. My lack of voice and rage covered anything good.

Barry Stevens in *Don't Push the River, It Flows by Itself* says to become fury until there is nothing left. To let all the emotions pass through like the inside of a boat hollowed out with fire.

Being my pure rage in a safe space cleanses me. Using my voice, I scream into the sky. Yelling into a pillow or beating the bed with a whiffle bat. Pounding my chest like a gorilla. And then crying and releasing. Owning it all. Only then I am free, and the rage becomes a whisper instead of a tornado directing my life.

I can learn to deal with my anger as things come up in the present instead of using it to annihilate my loved ones with pent-up fury never released. My upset becomes a reminder for me to keep my voice.

RAGE.

Waiting

I waited because I believed I was second
in life, in relationship, in love

patterns of waiting and placing myself after
eradicated possibilities of
intimacy and connectedness

waiting
waiting
waiting

frustration creeping
resentment steeping
giving away my power
anger building
vision blind
rage
bubbling
under
the
s
u
r
f   a
c
e

time to release it
and heal

The Girlfriend

eerie
to walk into this house
that once was mine

    how did i leave my stuff?
    why could my choices not include me?
    why did i treat myself as less then?
    why did i teach him so?

he is full
a family man
recreating what crumbled when i left

when in fact
he was with me before
yet the lenses did not fall away
until i could see on my own.

should i say you're welcome
to the new girl friend
who can spend time with precious children
who came from he and i?

was the sacrifice of the
marriage worth changing
my perceived view of giving them a father?
he was a father before
he is a father now
i guess it could not be the sacrifice of me
because i left

i am a leaver
a breaker of structure
and promises

the wash of loss tumbling through
leaves me
vulnerable with pain
finally looking at my choices
and being responsible for where i am

I'm sorry • forgive me • I love you • Thank you[1]

---

[2] From the Ho'oponopono mantra.

Spewing

not knowing, not caring

no desire to be pairing

with you in this paradigm, this treachery and daring

wondering at the spewing

venom flowing from your mouth

spitting out the past and creating this drought

I'm done with you now, you no longer haunt me

I will lie here chattering, shivering and wanting

and it doesn't matter, your monsters alive and inviting

I say no to your toxic negativity and blaming

I'm not your whipping girl for the naming

be gone with your hatred, your malice, your gnashing

your teeth biting armor so wicked and thrashing

the trap is unsprung as you look up in dread

this gremlin attaches to me through the voices in your head

I spiral and lunge to move away from the fear, knowing fully that I'm in control here

watching, observing your hatred and passion

side-stepping your rage, not daring, nor matching

visualizing a quilted blanket batting bouncing and lazy buffering the noise

feeling fine with my wholeness and holding onto my poise

I won't subscribe to your hell, your vortex and madness

your definition of the situation is sadness

knowing now I am immune to your spell

I have my own rage and won't take on yours as well

firing back, and releasing my fury, I will not consume yours, I have my own jury

I own my own feelings I have my own voice

thankfully I am learning I am healing with choice

Internal Battle

prickly heat, back chest heart
covered in swarms of
black and red ants
stinging every particle
on fire with the unknown
of vulnerability
self-absorbed internal voices
shouting in my head
ego screaming to survive and stay
stuck in the labyrinth of self-loathing
monster attacking everyone around
with my endless needs and defenses
annihilating rocks trees mountains
with my insidious power
spewing "you are not good enough either"
gasping lungs full no room for air
no voice too much voice
thrashing in a quagmire of
my own making

Stay!
I need you to stay
so I can suck you dry
immerse myself in your
solidity
enmesh into
your soul body mind
no boundaries floating in togetherness
content in the pattern of losing myself
so I don't have to be responsible
leeching onto your skin
internal organs a tasty treat
for my massive yearning hunger for connectedness

Go!
I need you to go far away into oblivion
so I don't have to think about you
I pull into myself, create boundaries again
overachieving by building barriers
taller than villages in the sky above mountains
to keep the
prickly bushes at bay
plunging into despair when you are gone
nauseous reeling from the disconnect
misery abounds doubts endless streaming
like video stuck in replay
isolate
    separate
        retreat
far into my corner of hell
demons nipping at my heels
maniacal laughter breathing, heaving in my ear
as my body fills with inadequacy
hidden rage
fear like an acrid bite of poison berries
puckering my tongue and choking

enough, I say, be gone!
I am done with this drama
allow only the rage to cleanse
the fury to mend
embracing essence, I touch my divine
cherishing self, I honor my choices
grateful for the wounds uncovered
shaking in relief that the storm is passing
expanded self-healing
wounds closing
cells rebuilding cycle of destruction and rebirth completing

what shall be created now?

17 Being

Residing in my body, i feel and become "Fernhead".

Experiencing living rather than thinking about living.

i am not my thoughts, beliefs or actions.

I am.

HS

BEING. How many of us are here but are not really present in our bodies? One of my tried and true escape mechanisms is to be far, far away, anywhere but in my body in this moment.

I do my best to maintain the practice of being present. I make eye contact with others and focus on listening to them. When I get side-tracked or distracted, I let the other know. "Hey," I say, "I wandered off, but I'm really interested in what you were saying. Can you please repeat?" I say this instead of pretending I was fully present and engaged all along.

I once saw a picture of a woman meditating, and where her head should have been, there was a fern. That's why I decided to call her "Fernhead" and use this coined word as a reminder to myself to quit thinking so much. Instead, I should be "Fernhead" and trust the flow of the universe. Trust that which is already there will unfold and manifest. And re-member that I am a unique expression of the universe.

Even though I may think I am my actions, my thoughts, and my beliefs, I am not. Allowing Fernhead to emerge is letting nature's intelligence express the greater truth within and through me. This happens when I stop thinking and allow the divine truth of my essence to emerge and be expressed.

When I was going to school, raising children, and working, I was always busy. It takes ongoing training to let go of my busyness and let myself be still. Sometimes I do activities that put me in my body, like going to a local drumming circle where we beat on our drums and feel the rhythm of aliveness in our bodies.

I continue to learn to breathe and acknowledge my physical body and honor my gifts. I'm learning to be fully present instead of jumping into my head or taking myself far away in speculation, regret, and mind chatter. I feel my clothes against my skin, listen to my breath moving my chest in and out, and press my feet against the cool tile. I am grateful as I acknowledge where I am at this moment.

BEING.

Fernhead

Be . . .

still

cease

thoughts

allow

myself to

place

a fern

instead

of

my

head

on

top

of

my

neck

Inanimate Object

black stapler
sits
inert

stationary solitary solid
tangible in its molecular structure
atoms seemingly frozen in form
unmoving to my mind's eye.

a reminder of this physical plane in which we exist.
a human being waiting resisting resolutely accepting
that which is

with purpose
we are

Deep Splash

days

long

hour

short

lines

increase as

crows walk across

the sand

(my face)

deep breath

splash

sparkling

water

surrounds

ubiquitous

coldness

thrill of

sensation

filling every shivery

molecule of my

overheated body

refreshed

Trees Know

leaves bantering and chattering
giving space for what they know
is to come

trees not trying to grow fast
a manifestation to be all one
no rush for the world
the rocks and trees stay solid

while we jester gesture grapple gasping gnashing
to try and discover meaning

when all the while
the tree
dwells
inside
us

the perfect
divinity
of sounds
resonating
resounding
residing
in
us

I Am Well

without movement
distracted by laundry for a moment
back to contemplating life and all its

glory
blessings abound with the silence

inanimate objects take on personalities
as I sit in the love seat and soak in the

colors
of life on the wall
deep burgundy paint
fills
me
to the core
green sea foam walls transport me to the water
seagulls chatter and dive below
the ocean tides recede and refill

timeless in the silence of the world
that goes on without regard to people or

their stuff

silence like a mountain, snow covered peak
strong and stoic

fills me up again to face the endless

chatter of society
and
know that I am well

Hematite

conscious of the unreal
    perceived surreal state
        that I am in

today wearing hematite earrings
    stones weighted
        polished palpably pulling
            me
                grounding
                in deep roots to
                    keep me present
                in this body

allowing my divinity
acknowledging yours

The Queen

these bones and cells
sinewy fibers strands of matter
purple blood pumping heart palpitations
souls (of feet) interlace with earth feeling grass prickly
as grasshoppers leap to the other side

microcosms of ants scurrying to feed their armies
divide and conquer to prolong the destiny of the tribe
sacrificing all to feed the great queen

feminine earth enveloping fiery core of volcanic masculine
in tandem together propelling the rotation of the planet with
reciprocity

root tendrils entwine with seeds of others
air twisting creating space for growth
water molecules seep into emersion
life giving forces of creation
manifesting a balance
of you and me

18 Integrating Forgiveness

All parts of me, light and dark are integrated.

I forgive myself.

Even when I forget, eventually I come back to acceptance, balance and forgiveness.

HS

INTEGRATING FORGIVENESS. I continue to learn how I create my world. If I build barriers, then I exist behind barriers. If I create safety, I live in safety. Learning that the love I receive is the love I believe I deserve. Loving without expectation of reciprocity.

In a "Radically Alive" workshop by Ann Bradney, I learned how closed I was to love. In one exercise, my partner and I had to face each other, look into each other's eyes and connect. Once we connected, my partner cried and wanted to hug me. His emotion and intensity felt overwhelming to me, so I yelled at him to get away. It took us some time to negotiate the space of what worked for both of us to feel connected, safe, and loved.

I was shocked to learn that my partner also needed my guidance on what was safe for him to do in order for him to help me to feel intimate with him. He was brave and generous in his loving and acceptance as I went back and forth on what worked for me. This also taught me that I have to tell people what I want. Communication and setting boundaries are two-way streets. It is balance.

I also learned to forgive myself (again) while playing Satori, the "radical forgiveness game." Just as my breath is released over and over, I have to release and forgive over and over. Fifty percent of our breathing is the inhale and fifty percent is the exhale. So half of our living is embracing, receiving, and taking in, and the other half is releasing, forgiving, clearing. I almost didn't put this section in this book because sometimes I forget to forgive myself.

INTEGRATING FORGIVENESS.

Sticks and Stones

I am learning
that the rhyme

    sticks
        and
           stones
can break my bones
but words will never hurt me

take a lot of work to be true

continually detaching from meaning
instead of replaying the ancient
internalized agreement of unworthiness

I no longer know what to say
or believe what I see in your eyes my eyes your eyes
wanting to honor self compassion
my views your views perspectives shared
and yet the fury of your pain my pain
overtakes dignity and reactivity sets in again

this perpetual surrender to not take personally
your words your hurt my words my hurt
knowing well the self-defenses behind the mask
understanding the voice you gain I gain is perceived self-worth
and
you don't want to be annihilated, either

choosing to keep my internal agreements of dignity and love
instead of engaging in ritual patterns of word slinging
is an arduous task
and gets easier
every day

Rank

so if you were happy
    where did I fit in?
        where did I rank in happiness?

    how would you have felt if I was unavailable all the time?
        perhaps I was..

    negated you all the time?
        perhaps I did...

how would it feel if I was blaming you for my unhappiness?
    perhaps sad and lonely

    my past was my present and my future
        perhaps we were too stuck to see

        my past didn't change, you heard me but
            perhaps we were not able to listen

        my present didn't change, you loved me
            but perhaps I couldn't hear

        layers of conflict
            can we be forgiven and forgive?

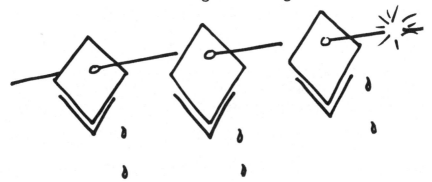

Divine Individuality

divine spark
  unique
in this life
body contained emotions spirit intellect
"Quadrinity of Self"[2]

W
I
C
K
sustaining
wax feeding
dancing tumbling
flaring flame of color
single light of blue
orange sparkling yellow
leaps in the stubble of
hot white tip blending to
black and red in its bed
of nurturing coals recomposing
to steaming embers
slumbering turning
to ash
zealously burning
who I am
allowing all
joyful grieving
grateful healing
complete with this
compilation that
I Am

---

[3] From the Quadrinity, Hoffman Process by Bob Hoffman

Teaching

his grieving tender wounds lacerated
with broken promises reach me
in distant echoes of
days past

knowing now
I have my own emotions, joys, fears
anger, responsibilities
life
to live

thank you for the teaching
I am sorry for the wounding

Human Webbing

fingers entwined, knees up
hopping in a whirl of human webbing
childhood game cracking the whip as I fly off the end of the line

solemnly stepping
a band of angels approaching
one by one easing
like tumbleweeds into
an earthly vessel
sacred meadows resound
with tones of spirits past
healing earth envelopes me
a womb of heartbeat drumming
a solace to release into the ground

new perspective precious child within
cradling this flower petal being
seeing my survival self
radiant willful deceitful
mischievous manipulative
all defenses to protect the little one
thank you, I say
thank you for my defenses
for keeping me alive when the defenses of others
consumed all in its wake
thank you for hiding fragility so I could survive

holding hands
cradling my vulnerable being
I dance now in unity with myself
lights and shadows integrated
into a whole self
choosing composite

19 Gratefulness

I choose it all.

I am grateful and I now know to honor my journey, your journey. Our journeys together.

HS

GRATEFULNESS. I am matter. I am breathing, with bones creating my structure, blood coursing through my veins, and living my unique purpose. I am a spiritual being encased in a physical form for this lifetime.

I am grateful for my feelings. I am grateful for my body. I am grateful for my intellect. I am grateful for the defenses that brought me to this point. I am grateful for my mistakes. I am grateful for my divinity.

I am great-full. I am great and I am full.

I am grateful for my children. I am grateful for my family. I am grateful for the father of my children, who is instrumental in my personal journey. I am grateful for my mother and my father.

I am grateful for my friends. I am grateful for the sweet air we breathe. I am grateful for the grocery clerk who smiles at me. I am grateful for the challenging personalities I meet that reflect parts of me that need to be revealed and healed.

I am grateful for poetry. When I read or hear it, I am reminded of who I am. Of my journey, my vulnerability, and that you and I are one.

I am grateful for learning that my emotions are my sensors. They allow me the experience of living.

I am grateful for the gift of life.

Being in the knowing that I choose everything, I choose patterns or I choose to go beyond.

GRATEFULNESS.

Flying

I Am

flying through
    the air
    mountain ranges lie
    nestled in shadows
    squares of brown and green

    cause me to ponder
    the significance of
    the whole and the
    smallness of myself

    drops of water
    splashed from the fountain
    into the ocean
    life beads of intention
      we each bring to the table.

    encounters
    assisting in
    consciousness on this
    journey that is evolving
      not an end

    I am healing

She (High Priestess)

She walks in me, I deny
She breathes in me, I protest

how to claim the power that
we are all born with?

the divine high priestess self within
covered by years of neglect and abuse
patterns of reactive unconscious living

sparks of light glimmer
flicker, sputter and go out
or perhaps it is just another view
to unwrap the chatter and let go
of the void of negating self

She lives in me, I see
She shines in me, I feel
compassion for the
vulnerable child woman strong bending growing
integrating relaxing
with the winds of the journey beautiful

I am She

Embracing

embracing

my life of dreams

living in joy

feeling beauty

consciousness

must be present

no more stuckness

or voices of yesterday

nor the uncertainty

of tomorrow

continually practicing the Four Agreements

---

[4] *The Four Agreements*, by Don Miguel Ruiz

Sacred Female Warrior

take off the armor, gold-plated
solid unyielding
loosen the garb of many layers
fluidity and flexibility
releasing all fear
release... release...
an act of continuous motion
relearn
let go
let life flow through my veins
with unattached splendor

as I trust what the universe has to offer

invite accept receive
relinquish the myriad
celebrations
losses
joys
conversations encountered
in a single rotation of 86400 seconds
individual instants in time
ticking away in this mortal body
each breath a cycle of
life death life inherent

as I remember

the essence of being

and my divinity
a sacred warrior embracing life
naked in my vulnerability

Perhaps

perhaps..
God is
    expansion, allowing
       all things

perhaps..
I am
  healing, vulnerable, full of masks
  of darkness, deceit, and denial

perhaps..
I am
    light, barriers, full of hope laughter and cherishing

I honor myself and my quest for
excellence in every area of my life.

I am divine
I Am

A Breath

I am
    a breath
  I learn

        crumbling illusions, trembling, mirroring, open
expanding
    contracting

grateful churning yearning
living whirling
curling in
this
snapshot sliver of
possibility
time frame
that bonds you and me

20 Choices

Each moment is simple, a yes or no option.

Sometimes I forget, so I go back to being Fernhead and release attachment (again).

I choose.

HS

CHOICES. We always have a simple yes or no choice. Sometimes I make things complicated when I forget about being and choosing the voices in my head over choosing happiness.

If life is made of choices, then do I always pick my environment?

How sad that I make choices that cause me suffering, and how liberating it is that I am making the choice.

If I accept my situation, I am making a choice, even if I believe I have no control. A friend was falling off a ladder and he chose to fall as soon as he realized he had slipped and was in motion. His choosing allowed him to relax into his falling instead of resisting, which made him less tense during the fall and his injuries were much less than they might have been.

Knowing that I choose everything, I choose patterns or I choose to go beyond. Paraphrasing a quote shared by my teacher Susan Austin-Crumpton, when we are fully engaged in our life situation we become fully alive. I choose aliveness.

Once I was informed of a pending layoff and told that I was likely on the list and would lose my job. After my initial panic, I accepted the situation and decided that although I couldn't control the bean counters, I could control how I worked while their decisions were being made. So I released the fear, accepted the possibility of no control and no job, and decided that if I lost my job, the universe would provide.

I choose to believe that there is purpose in my being here. In your being here. I choose to believe there is meaning in life.

CHOICES.

Today's Walk

choices of

today

negate

the antiquated

mode

of the

past

a daily walk

A Daily Choice

A daily choice to live

A daily choice to be married
    or not

A daily choice to work

A daily choice to spend time with
    my children

A daily choice to live life to
    its fullest

A daily choice to smile and
    be thankful for my blessings

A daily choice to communicate
    my needs to my partner so he can also
have conscious choices in
    whether or not to travel the same path

A daily choice to engage
    instead of watching television in a stupor

A daily choice to write my
    thoughts without censorship
    for fear that someone will
    read them and pass judgment

A daily choice to
    be creative

A daily choice to enrich my
    life with beauty and love

A daily choice to experience
being surrounded
    by positive people open to opportunity

A daily choice to let others
know that I need to be
    cherished

A daily choice to wake up in
the morning, ready for the
adventure ahead

A daily choice to drop off
the pretenses and baggage
of things past over which I have
no control anyway

A daily choice to confront issues
as they arise instead of
letting my integrity be
    bartered for the comfort of others

A daily choice to actively
define myself
on a minute-by-minute basis

A daily choice to work hard,
play hard, and to be a good mother

A daily choice to be my
highest authentic self

A daily choice to realize that
I must reach out to others

A daily choice to not punish
  my partner or myself for who and what we are

A daily choice to be accepting of
  myself and others

A daily choice to release control and
  trust the highest purpose

A daily choice to quit battling
  on every single issue

A daily choice to be in
  full relationship

A daily choice to connect
  with those around me and
  not shut myself off because
  they don't respond the way
  I want them to

A daily choice to be kind

A daily choice to think about
  and have sexual relations

A daily choice to accept
  that sex is natural and healthy

A daily choice to be choosy and selective
  about who I choose to spend
    my time and body with

A daily choice to set my boundaries with each moment

A daily choice to flow and be Fernhead

21 Releasing

My breathing is a model for releasing.

The exhalation of my breath is half of the breathing cycle and half of my life.

Releasing is just as important as breathing in.

HS

RELEASING. With every breath we inhale and take in, we also exhale and release. We inhale sweet nourishing air, we exhale toxin and poison.

Releasing is half of our breath and half of our life.

When I first discovered that we are never done, I was disappointed. I thought grownups had everything figured out. Even knowing we are ever evolving, it is difficult to let go. I still want to believe a certain way. I want to hold on to my emotions and my blaming and my criticisms. I want people and situations to be exactly as I want them.

Once I knew a man who wanted to connect with me. But he had no boundaries (and in hind-sight, clearly neither did I). Engaging with him left me feeling engulfed by his emotions and expectations (another great mirror of myself). I began to react with rage whenever he started to talk to me. Then I learned that it is I who need to change by holding boundaries and releasing any expectation that he will be different from who he is. I have to let go of my idea that I can shape his behavior by my rage. I have to accept (again) that he is who he is and acknowledge that it is different from what I want reality to be. I have to release again. And release again. And release again.

I release in order to bring in more. This is the cycle of life and death. Releasing what no longer serves creates a clear, clean path for the journey ahead. Just as a warrior of life releases emotional attachment and trusts the universe, I also release.

RELEASING.

Garage Sale

as observer,

  I gaze

    feeling with

  abstract

clarity

     pieces of my life

      float

       away

        into another's

      universe.

sifted and sorted

  lives now touched by

    my energy

trapped in things of the past

gone

  for a dollar

College Cycle

piles of clothes
   lie empty on the floor
     a reminder of the child
   that once was in this place

no longer cursing the clothing carelessly dropped
     tripping over
       gentle reminder of
         voices loud
           laughing poking fun
             with friends sharing
               floor space crowded
                 sprawled on couches with feet
                         dangling
                     over

frantically staying busy to keep the loneliness at bay
allowing the grieving as my children have gone away

finally releasing and being comfortable within
     and in two weeks they'll be home again
cycle of joy gladness weariness begins anew with
fresh piles of laundry in front of the stair
   dropped as if to say
     I'm still here
heart full and complete knowing how very soon
   precious feet
      will make their journey to the door
      as they launch to create lives of their own

Pink Goo

energy in
   moving out
  once again
  1, 2, 3
  1, 2, 3

dance steps take over
   reminiscent of life
  structure
is present maybe once
maybe thrice

patterns not facing
the inevitable belief
society whining
it feigns the relief

staying and smouldering
suffocation galore
not in the least
not in the past

to release..
therein
lies the door

glowing
and twirling
tondue and swirl

floor changing
sky dancing
as the structure
unfurls

it's cloak rearranging
transforming amazing

small world
  facing
    out
    arms open
and floating
air currents
unseen

  higher
    and
      lighter
perhaps it's a dream

carried on currents
  as a feather
    it seems
  one way then another
      no direction
it gleans
  questing for truth
    translucent and clean
      spiraling lilting
pink gold and blue sheen

  up to the sky
    away high and by
  traveling in a
pink plastic bubble
that

PoPs

leaving goo on the table

We Carried

knowing now
    your sarcasm
    pain
    spewing of anger
was
your only way to
    gain a voice
      because
        you hurt
    and had to
erect
many
barriers

as did I

it will take us some time
to let go of what we carried

22 Joyfulness

I am joyfully nurturing and feeding my soul.

My awareness is expanded.

I am you and you are me.

JOYFULNESS. Allowing joyful nurturing and finding what feeds my soul. Expanding my awareness on my path.

I become childlike and wake up feeling alive. This is the only body I know. This is my life. I am my full self, expanding and contracting. I am great-full.

I release expectations and outcomes again and again and connect with those around me with intimacy, love, and respect.

I don't have to attach to any single emotion, and I know that even joy is not forever. I am joyful one moment and sad the next, and irritated the next. I am a fluid vessel rather than a dried, stuck block of clay. And even with the myriad emotions flowing, I am quietly joyful in my being that all is well.

I am free to be who I am and I am still learning who that is. I am one facet of the human experience and I am everyone.

I am you and you are me.

JOYFULNESS.

Whole

I am passion I am quiet
I am fire I am stillness

laughter and sorrow
simultaneously

full
empty

playful
serious

joyful
  whole
    complete

enough

Pirouettes

sand in my hair, my teeth
eyes
stinging
the wind
from the sea

gritty and warm with cold underneath
toes crunching wet
standing still creates a bowl of water
for minnows to dive in
I teeter
off balance

ocean's rhythms
refill
and renew
constant
changing
retract
and
return
covering the sand
and our marks
of temporary discovery

bringing reality back to life
breathe in
breathe out

a series of pirouettes
makes me dizzy
I fall and laugh at the
joy of being alive

Flexibility

delicious delight
world of dreams

is all that we see
just a dream within a dream?

controlled by whom?
the inside or out
knowing not where it starts
the vision the doubts

environments
changing
flexibility is the key
living life to its fullest
and daring to be
me

Cycles

daily
I walk
change
grow
feel
hurt
heal
love
withdraw
recharge
come back

and
breathe
in this life

Feast

suspended
motion
slows
time
pieces
as I embrace
the present
joyful
in my
independence
free of expectations
loyalties defined
myself
at the top
of
the
list

outcomes
natural
not wielded
through tenuous
control of
others
instead
fully responsible

side affects
enjoying the moment
adding spice
of course
as I feast
upon
this life

Connected

I love my children

I love my choices

I love myself

thankful for

unconditional love

of my family

I am glad to

have them back

Coming Up Unstuck

percolating
marinating
deep in the journey
purposeful
divinity
reveals

grieving
leaving
coming up unstuck
exhilarating life
no longer concealed

brushing layers away
clearing old peat moss and stuff
allowing divine gifts to blossom
believing songs of enough
sharing revealing
ecstatically
building
intimacy
yearnings
anew

glad for the journey
the breaking of me
possibilities
and choosing
to bloom

Threshold of Change

I stand at the

threshold of change

anticipating

the Pavlov effect

when the freedom

of it all strikes me

to my core

and I fly into

the clouds

Joyful

HS

Resources

There are hundreds of modalities and healing methods. Here are some that worked for me. Many best wishes in finding what works for you.

Some processes, workshops, and educational programs

Celebrating Men and Satisfying Women, workshop created by Allison Armstrong, http://www.understandmen.com

The Estuary, Auric Healing, the School of Healing Arts, Susan Austin-Crumpton, http://theschoolofhealingarts.com

The Hoffman Process, Hoffman Institute Foundation, https://www.hoffmaninstitute.org

Landmark Education (Curriculum for Living and the Team Management and Leadership Program), http://www.landmarkworldwide.com

Elements of Natural Rhythms, Lisa Michaels, http://lisa-michaels.com

The Priestess Process, created by Nicole Christine, Facilitated by Carol Rydell in Kansas City, KS.

Radical Aliveness Institute, Ann Bradney, http://radicalaliveness.org

Some healers/facilitators

Susan Austin-Crumpton, *Auric Energy: Core Energetics* Therapist, http://theestuary.org/susan-austin-crumpton

Sam Austin, *Shaman*, http://heartofthehealer.org/pmt-thoth-teachers

Dr. Bill Bird, *Imago* Therapist, http://www.drsbird.com

Ann Bradney, *Radical Aliveness: Core Energetics,* Therapist and workshop leader. http://www.eomega.org/workshops/teachers/ann-bradney

Dr. Pamela Chubbuck, *Vitally Alive: Core Energetics* Therapist, http://vitallyalive.com/

Lisa Michaels, *Natural Rhythms*, http://lisa-michaels.com/

Suzy Newman, *Auric Energy: Core Energetics* Therapist,
http://theestuary.org/suzy-newman/

Dr. Wendy and Dr. Bob Patterson, *Imago* Therapists,
https://perkinsit.securesites.net/ relationshipcoaching.net/about.html

Lisa Inanna, *BEST (Bio-Energetic Synchronistic Technique)* Practitioner.
http://www.lisainanna.com/

Some Books

Andreas, Brian. *Mostly True Collected Stories & Drawings.* Story People,
September 1998.

Armstrong, Alison. *Queen's Code.* PAX Programs, Inc., 2013.

Armstrong, Alison. *Keys to the Kingdom. The Development Stages of Men.*
PAX Programs, Inc., 2003.

Brown, Brene. *Gifts of Imperfection.* Center City, MN: Hazelden Publishing, 2010.

Brown, Brene. *Daring Greatly.* New York: Gotham Books, 2012.

Estes, Clarissa Pinkola. *Women Who Run with the Wolves: Myths and
Stories of the Wild Woman Archetype.* New York: Ballantine, 1992.

Hendrix, Harville. *Getting the Love You Want,* rev. ed. New York: Henry
Holt & Co, 2007.

Johnson, Robert A. *He: Understanding Masculine Psychology,* rev. ed.
New York: Harper Perennial, 1989.

Johnson, Robert A. *She: Understanding Feminine Psychology,* rev. ed.
New York: Harper Perennial, 1989.

Johnson, Robert A. *We: Understanding the Psychology of Romantic Love.*
New York: HarperOne, 2009.

Keen, Sam. *Fire in the Belly: On Being a Man.* New York: Bantam Books, 1992.

Kidd, Sue Monk. *Dance of the Dissident Daughter: A Woman's Journey from
Christian Tradition to the Sacred Feminine.* New York: HarperOne, 2006.

Kirshenbaum, Mira. *Too Good to Leave, Too Bad to Stay: A Step-by-Step
Guide to Help You Decide to Stay In or Get Out of Your Relationship.*
New York: Plume, 1997.

Lerner, Harriet. *The Dance of Intimacy: A Woman's Guide to Courageous
Acts of Change in Key Relationships.* New York: Harper Perennial, 1997.

Lerner, Harriet. *Dance of Anger: A Woman's Guide to Changing the Patterns of Intimate Relationships.* New York: William Morrow, 2014.

Lerner, Harriet. *The Dance of Deception: A Guide to Authenticity and Truth-Telling in Women's Relationships.* New York, William Morrow, 1997.

Mason, Paul and Randi Kreger. *Stop Walking on Eggshells: Taking Your Life Back When Someone You Love Has Borderline Personality Disorder.* Oakland, CA: New Harbinger Publications, 2010.

McWilliams, Peter, Harold H. Broomfield, and Melba Colgrove. *How to Survive the Loss of a Love.* Los Angeles: Prelude Press, 1993.

Meenach, Kathy. *Sojourns.* Heron Lee Publication, Inc. 2009.

Michaels, Lisa. *Natural Rhythms: A Sacred Guide into Nature's Creation Secrets.* CreateSpace, 2014.

Myss, Caroline. *Anatomy of the Spirit: The Seven Stages of Power and Healing.* New York: Harmony Books, 1997.

Pipher, Mary and Ruth Ross. *Reviving Ophelia, Saving the Selves of Adolescent Girls.* New York: Riverhead, 2005.

Ruiz, Don Miguel. *The Four Agreements: A Practical Guide to Personal Freedom (A Toltec Wisdom Book).* San Rafael, CA: Amber-Allen Publishing, 1997.

Shaef, Anne Wilson. *Women's Reality: An Emerging Female System.* New York: HarperOne, 1992.

Sheehy, Gail. *Passages: Predictable Crisis of Adult Lives.* New York: Ballantine, 2006.

Singer, Michael. *The Untethered Soul: The Journey Beyond Yourself.* Oakland, CA: New Harbinger Publications, 2007.

Stevens, Barry. *Don't Push the River, It Flows by Itself.* Lafayette, CA: Real People Press, 1970

Thesenga, Susan and Eva Pierrakos. *The Undefended Self, Living the Pathwork.* Madison, VA: Pathwork Press, 2001.

Vanzant, Iyanla. *In the Meantime: Finding Yourself and the Love You Want.* New York: Touchstone, 1999.

Wheeler, CPA Robert Wm.. *The Money Nerve: Navigating the Emotions of Money.* Bloomington, IN: Balboa Press, 2013.

Some Poets

Sabra Bowers, https://sabrabowers.wordpress.com/

Charles Bukowsi, http://bukowski.net/poems/

David Whyte, http://www.davidwhyte.com/poetry.html

Some Music and CDs

Henry Scott, *Whole... Not Perfect, The Blue Flannel CD*
www.HylanArt.com, or www.cdbaby.com/Artist/HenryScott

Alanis Morissette, *Jagged Little Pill, Former Infatuation Junkie*, and *Under Rug Swept*

Sara Mclachlan, *Fumbling towards Ecstasy*

Dave Mathews, *Crash*

Linkin Park, *Hybrid Theory, Meteora*

Incubus, *Make Yourself*

Pink Floyd, *Animals, The Wall*

Sia, *Breathe Me*

Jeff Craft, Beginning Meditations: Expanding Peace
www.amazon.com/Beginning-Meditations-Expanding-Jeff-Craft

Jeff Craft, Living With Awareness: Tantric Meditations
for Expanded Conscious Living
www.amazon.com/Living-Awareness-Meditations-Expanded-Conscious

A video

Brene Brown's TED Talk on Vulnerability,
http://www.ted.com/talks/brene_brown_on_vulnerability?language=en

A game

Satori (Game of Awareness and Radical Forgiveness),
www.radicalforgiveness.com/the-game

Some tools and practices around healing and conscious living

Therapy

Supportive network of family and friends

Acceptance of what is and what is not

Meditation

Body movement and dance, practices to be in your body

Acceptance of self

Retreats

Personal growth

Reading about other people's journeys

Doing things you love

Practicing the Four Agreements

Five stages of grief[5]

Denial

Anger

Bargaining

Depression

Acceptance

---

[5] From *On Grief and Grieving: Finding the Meaning of Grief Through the Five Stages of Loss* by Elizabeth Kübler-Ross and David Kessler.

Final notes

The gift of a treadmill trekked into my basement after the divorce.
He was still trying to take care of me.

A special thank you to the girlfriend. She takes care of the man I first
loved and the father of our children. They now partner in creating a
loving environment that eluded my former husband and I as we
danced in a marriage without tools. I am grateful for her and our
blended families.

Compromising to have a fair outcome versus compromise of our very
integrity are two totally different views. Honor self and others with
our agreements.

Practice vigilant self-care. Thank you, David from RAI, and David from
Paris.

It is about how we choose to live our lives and honor our agreements.

Wishing you well on your journey; I am glad to be on mine.
Fair winds and safe travels.

Author's Biography

LISA YVONNE is grateful to be the mother of two adult children, whom she loves beyond words. Lisa is a poet, lover of words, life adventures, and thrives when traveling and exploring the world. It has taken her a lifetime to learn to integrate her logical engineering self with her free spirit dancing self.

Lisa strives for personal growth and is committed to healing in the world, starting with everyone and daily personal choices.

She is grateful for the personal journey that led to the creation of this book, and hopes that others may find the tools and support needed as they search for answers.

Artist's Biography

HENRY SCOTT was born in 1966 in Savannah, Georgia. His family moved to the small town of Conyers (20 miles east of Atlanta) when he was six weeks old, and there he grew to be a young man. At the age of 18, he escaped the small town and went on a 13-year quest traveling through the United States, Canada, and Central Europe as a performer, director, and choreographer. As he traveled, he searched for meaning and purpose in the seemingly banal and superficial world. His quest, like most quests, ended where it had begun... back in the small town of Conyers. The last 18 years have been spent teasing apart his family history, healing, and making sense of his place in the world.

Doodling has been a source of sanity for Henry: the pad and the pen are reliable friends and allies on his journey. His drawings are explorations of the internal life made manifest on the page by way of stream of consciousness drawing. The drawings reveal themselves to him one line at a time and usually end up in unexpected and transformative places.

Many Thanks to the Book Creation Team

HENRY SCOTT, ARTIST AND MUSICIAN Henry, who you are in the world, your art and music are unparalleled self-expressions of unity, wholeness and healing. Thank you for your friendship and for your beautiful contribution to this book.

GARRISON BROOKS, GRAPHIC DESIGNER Thank you for propelling this project to the next level by digitizing the artwork for this book from pen and paper to eformat. Your enthusiasm for the poetry and art, and your invaluable feedback helped me realize this book could augment bookshelves of those already in healthy relationships.

BARBARA ARDINGER, PH. D., EDITOR Thank you for your humor, your professionalism and for 'getting it' immediately. Your feedback and review are appreciated.

SHAWN MORNINGSTAR, BOOK DESIGN/LAYOUT Thank you, Shawn, for your incredible work. Your vision, enthusiasm and support are the binding energies which are bringing the last pieces of this dream to fruition.

MICHAEL TANAMACHI, COVER ARTIST Thank you Michael for your listening and creating the perfect thought-provoking book cover and design.

PETER BOWERMAN *The Well-Fed Self-Publisher.* Peter, thank you for your valuable consultation sessions, title contribution, and professional contacts in the publishing business to bring this book to completion with excellence.

And to the many friends and family who believed in me, reviewed, provided feedback, and supported me throughout this journey.

Where to buy Coming Up Unstuck

www.ComingUpUnstuck.com

www.comingupunstuck.com/get-your-book

Where to buy Henry's Art

www.HylanArt.com

www.HylanArt.com/get-your-art

Contact Fernhead Publishing, LCC for group discounts

info@FernheadPublishing.com

Follow Lisa's travel blog at:

www.FernheadTravels.com